MAELMIN

An Archaeological Guide

Clive Waddington

illustrations by David Hall

CS Publishing

Maelmin

First published 2001
ISBN 0 9530163 5 8

Published by:
CS Publishing, Main Road, Milfield, Wooler,
Northumberland, NE71 6JD
Tel: +44 (0) 1668 216535

The Maelmin Heritage Trail acknowledges the generous support of our sponsors:

This project has been
part financed by the
European Community
(European Regional
Development Fund)

UNIVERSITY OF
NEWCASTLE UPON TYNE

ENGLISH HERITAGE
No one does **more** for England's heritage

contents

Introduction

Milfield is surrounded by ancient henge monuments which date back to 2000BC.

For decades archaeologists have researched these sacred sites making discoveries which enable us to peer into the daily life of our ancestors.

The henge at Maelmin is a reconstruction based on the Milfield North Henge, excavated in 1975-7.

The Till valley is a landscape of steep hills, meandering rivers, forested denes, rocky crags and a fertile valley floor. Although now a largely agricultural landscape the rich lowland fields and bleak moorland hills hide the remains of a fascinating ancient past.

The landscape was home to some of the earliest inhabitants of northern Britain; later it was monumentalised as a sacred valley with one of the largest henge and rock art complexes by the first farming communities; the Iron Age Votadini tribe constructed one of their great hillfort capitals here and after escaping the ravages of Roman occupation some say Arthur gave battle here. A century later the greatest king of Northumbria, Edwin, introduced Christianity to the north at his royal town at Yeavering and in later centuries the landscape bore witness to some of the greatest Anglo-Scottish battles, the fierce fighting of the Wars of the Roses and sieges of its medieval castles culminating in one of history's turning points at the battle of Flodden Field. Since then the landscape played backdrop to the lawlessness of the border reivers before emerging at the forefront of developments in English agriculture during the age of improvement. With the age of steam the railway came to the valley pursuing one of the most picturesque routes in the land snaking around the north face of the Cheviot hills through Glendale.

With the militarisation of Europe and the expansionist zeal of the fascist states the world was sucked into war bringing an airfield, pillboxes, anti-aircraft batteries and magazines to the valley.

The landscape of the Till Valley is shrouded in the archaeological remains of distant times bearing testament to the rich variety of past human experience that has been etched on the land. The remains vary from upstanding buildings and structures, to low humps and bumps in the ground, from buried features invisible at ground level to stray finds of single artefacts lying on a field surface. However, these remains are not merely isolated finds sitting mute in the land but rather the material objects and structures that allow us to touch our ancestors and experience their physical world. Moreover, by visiting the remains of our ancestors we can do more than simply access their tactile world - we can also experience their sense of place.

The relationship between people and the land they inhabit has profound importance for the way people view themselves within the world and in the way they exploit their environment. Changes in the way societies engaged with the landscape can be seen during different periods in the past. For example hunter-gatherers during the Mesolithic chose not to build monuments or subdue their landscape with human creations but rather to live a mobile and free existence as a part of the environment relying on hunting, fishing and gathering, in concert with the seasons.

Around 4000BC attitudes changed and people started to impose on the landscape by building the first permanent structures. These consisted of large burial mounds and ceremonial monuments which became increasingly elaborate. This move towards controlling the environment was also given expression by the domestication of plants

The Henge Builders (from left to right), back row: Paul Gething (archaeologist), Richard Chamberlain (history teacher), Ben Johnson (archaeologist), Sean Marsden (builder), Richard Aldous (wood carver), Sarah Groves (archaeology student), Phil Jansen (medical doctor), Andy Bates (leatherworker), Dr Clive Waddington. Front row: Vicky Bolderson (archaeologist), Hannah Lynch (archaeology student) and Eleanor Johnson (archaeologist).

and animals so that resources could be harvested from the landscape in a more controlled and predictable way.

By the Bronze Age technological innovations meant that metal could be extracted from the ground and not only did farming become more intensive but it also extended to its highest altitudinal limits at over 400m in the Cheviot hills. With the widespread construction of field boundaries and permanent houses for full sedentary farming communities by around 1600BC the concept of owning land and property appears to have become established.

During the Iron Age people's relationship with the landscape took yet another turn with the construction of elaborate fortified enclosures, usually in the most prominent places in the landscape. These hillforts were situated to dominate the surrounding area providing a symbol of the power and authority of the social elites who occupied these sites. By this time vast tracts of forest had been cleared, field systems laid out across upland and lowland and a hierarchy of settlements had emerged with homesteads, hamlets, villages and towns.

From an untamed wildwood which people dwelled in, the relationship people had with the landscape had changed, to become an ordered agricultural environment, which landowning people dwelled on.

The Mesolithic
(10000-4000BC)

By the end of the postglacial period around 10,000BC the lake, situated in what is now the floodplain, had drained away through the gorge at Etal and the polar front had retreated further north bringing a more temperate climate to much of Britain. With the increase in temperatures new kinds of plants and trees were able to colonise the landscape. The pine and birch woodland started to give way to a more varied flora which included oak, elm, willow, alder, hazel and lime, amongst other species. This rich vegetation provided by the broad-leaf forests, together with the warmer climate, was able to sustain a wider range, and greater number of, animal species than before. The arrival of wild cattle, wild pig and brown bear, as well as greater stocks of fish, fowl, small mammals and birds made the Milfield landscape a place of plenty and an attractive living space for humans.

One of the main features of the Mesolithic, or 'middle stone-age', is the change from an arctic tundra landscape through boreal forest to temperate broad-leaf forest - the native wildwood of Britain. The Mesolithic people had to change their way of life and subsistence strategies to cope with these fundamental changes to the landscape. The heavy arctic fur clothing of the first hunters became lighter while changes in the flint tool kit indicates the development of new types of hunting points for spears and arrows to catch the new range of prey available. The seasonal availability of resources also changed with winter shortages probably less severe. The new plant life meant nuts, berries and forest fruits could be collected while certain wild grasses and green-leaf plants could also be eaten. Meat, fish and some plant foods could be smoked or dried to keep, while honey, bark sap and duck eggs added greater nutrition and variety to the diet.

Once an animal had been caught, either by snare or hunted down with stone-tipped arrows and spears, a sharp flint flake was used to gut and skin the animal. Experiment during the construction of the Maelmin Heritage Trail have shown that a small roe deer can be

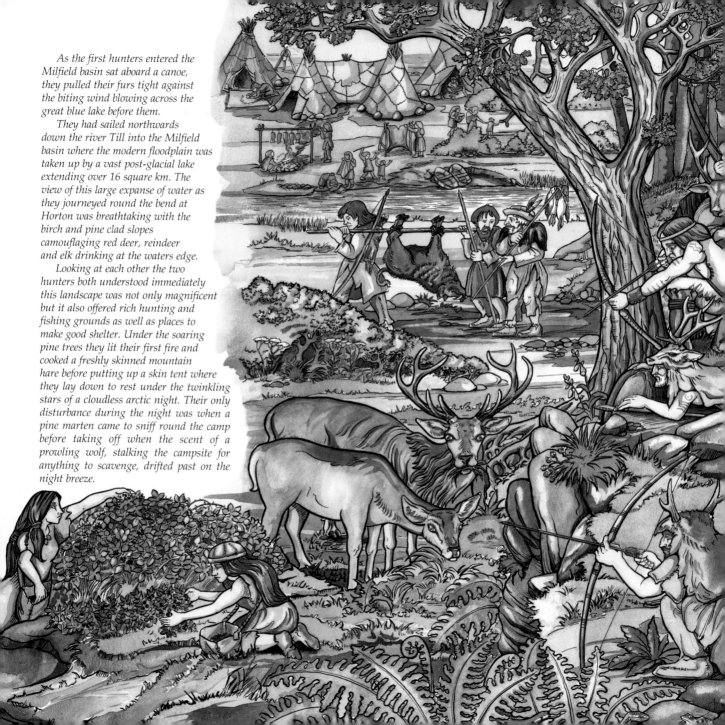

As the first hunters entered the Milfield basin sat aboard a canoe, they pulled their furs tight against the biting wind blowing across the great blue lake before them.

They had sailed northwards down the river Till into the Milfield basin where the modern floodplain was taken up by a vast post-glacial lake extending over 16 square km. The view of this large expanse of water as they journeyed round the bend at Horton was breathtaking with the birch and pine clad slopes camouflaging red deer, reindeer and elk drinking at the waters edge.

Looking at each other the two hunters both understood immediately this landscape was not only magnificent but it also offered rich hunting and fishing grounds as well as places to make good shelter. Under the soaring pine trees they lit their first fire and cooked a freshly skinned mountain hare before putting up a skin tent where they lay down to rest under the twinkling stars of a cloudless arctic night. Their only disturbance during the night was when a pine marten came to sniff round the camp before taking off when the scent of a prowling wolf, stalking the campsite for anything to scavenge, drifted past on the night breeze.

skinned in less than 10 minutes using only a sharp flint flake. The deer were butchered so that all their body parts were used: meat for eating, bone and antler for tools, sinew for thread, brain for tanning, hide for tents and making leather shoes and clothes. Finds of deer head-dresses with their antlers still attached, from a lake-side site in North Yorkshire, suggests hunting rituals to the spirit of deer took place. Such rituals may have included honouring the deer for giving up its life to provide the hunters and their families with the food and other resources they needed to live.

The distinctive tool type of the Mesolithic is the microlith (meaning "small-stone"), which formed the barbs and points for hunting weapons such as arrows and spears. Another common stone tool of this period is the scraper - frequently used for preparing skins by rubbing off the flesh. The Mesolithic groups of the Till valley used a wide variety of locally available stones to make tools including coloured agates, chert and quartz as well as flint brought from the Northumberland coast and more distant regions such as north-east Yorkshire.

Our hunter-gatherer ancestors, by now looking out on to a marshy wetland flood plain, surrounded by drier ground and forested hills, lived a free and unfettered existence content with life following the rhythm of the natural world.

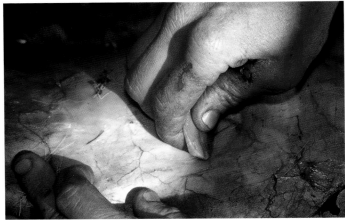

Using small flints to scrape away flesh from the deer skin is an essential first stage in the process of preparing hides.

These tools are very efficient and our ancestors would have been highly skilled in this type of work.

The Neolithic
(4000BC-2000BC)

After centuries of contact with people who travelled through the Milfield landscape the Mesolithic groups had heard about communities on the other side of the north sea who farmed land, lived in permanent houses all year round, made pottery, wore woollen clothes, valued prestigious possessions, built monuments and worshipped different gods. Contemptuous of these materialists who thought they could tame the world the hunter-gatherers shunned this way of life for their own ways which had served them well since time began.

Eventually, after a few years of poor weather when people were struggling to survive another winter, some members of the group realised they could gain considerable advantage by farming some land as it would help ensure a more predictable food supply all year round. Many of the young members of the tribe thought this was good and occasionally imitated the customs and dress of the farmer groups before being knocked to the floor and chastised by their elders. At a council of headmen these issues were discussed for the umpteenth time and then the leader spoke, "It is decided: we shall plant grain and tether animals but only to nurture from the land that which we need. We shall keep our gods and ancestral lore but honour them with symbols of our new way of living. No foreigner from outside the valley shall till this soil or claim the animals that we subdue. We will continue to hunt, gather and fish, moving our camps seasonally as we always have. And this, our tribal meeting ground, will be returned to as always for our yearly festivals. Let our efforts be dedicated to the universal spirit."

Areas of forest were cleared for cultivation and cattle, pig and sheep were captured for domestication. Clay was brought from the river beds and mixed with sand to make pots while stone axes were produced by grinding and polishing the local volcanic andesite. As time went by the stone axe, which was widely used for the felling of trees, became a potent symbol of the taming of the wildwood, and therefore, this new way of life. When the tribal leader died the headmen came together and discussed the great changes he had brought about, the lack of shortages over the winter months and also the impending encroachment of other tribes into their rich and fertile valley. It was decided to honour the headman by raising a

10

A break in the weather allows the team to set to work. Using basic tools they scrape away at the compacted sub-soil. The earth removed from the ditch is carried a short distance to form the outer bank. Inset: Richard Aldous at work carving one of the two entrance posts.

The completed henge is 33 metres in diameter with 21 outer posts and a ring of 30 inner posts. Earth from the inner ditches was used to form the outer bank. Henges range in size from 17m to 427m although the reconstructed example is typical for the region. Based on the time taken by the team to

Cutting up apples with flint tools the team cooks were able to provide a warming meal of stewed apples. Inset: Eleanor serving.

Hannah and Sarah undertake cooking duties. Damp wood meant a lot of smoke and food laced with ash and charcoal.

that we tended to eat about five or six meals a day but each was smaller than a modern meal. This allowed for people to last longer doing physical jobs as well as keeping up morale and feeding genuine, rather than routine, hunger.

Eleanor, with the help of Hannah and Sarah, did a fantastic job making food for thirteen people with utensils, equipment and foodstuffs often very alien to modern living. We encountered real problems with the fire as there was a massive shortage of dry and burnable wood as the incessant rain had saturated the woodland and the wind blew smoke and heat away from the fire.

This meant we couldn't have fires in the shelters as they would have smoked everyone out. We did, however, resort to bringing in hot embers in pottery vessels to provide some heat and light during the long evenings.

A scene of bronze age life showing smiths at work smelting copper and tin to make bronze.

Molten bronze is poured into stone moulds to make cast bronze tools and weapons.

The moustached man in the left foreground is hafting a flanged axe while the man at the front is admiring his rivetted dagger.

As well as weapons fine ornaments were produced, sometimes in precious metals such as gold and silver. The gold bands worn around the neck are called lunulae.

Iron Age
(700BC-AD43)

The Iron Age saw the continuation of the trends witnessed during the Bronze Age with social organisation becoming increasingly complex and, with time, the merging together of clan-based chiefdoms into regional kingdoms.

By the time the Romans came to Britain the Till valley lay in the kingdom of the Votadini. The British tribesman of the Iron Age, sometimes referred to as "Celts", belonged to a warrior-based society led by royal dynasties. A complex class structure developed with the warriors and druids below the king, then artisans and craftsmen together with the farming majority and an underclass of slaves. Warfare was highly specialised and included the brave woad-painted war frenzied warriors who went into battle naked, with erections, wielding mighty swords. There were also regular infantry, cavalry and charioteers. The infantry included sword and spear groups as well as archers, slingers and, for the nobles, their own shield bearers.

People lived in stone and wood-built roundhouses with thatched conical roofs, some situated in farmyards with connecting paddocks and fields while others were situated inside hillforts and others simply open sites. A settlement hierarchy is clearly evidenced in the archaeological record with settlement types ranging from single homesteads, to hamlets, villages and towns.

However, the defining settlements of the Iron Age were the great fortresses, often situated on the highest ground, known as hillforts. These grand fortifications were often built as earthworks with high banks and deep ditches in lowland areas and stone-built walls with rock-cut ditches in upland areas. The earthworks and stone ramparts were often surmounted by substantial timber palisades with a fighting platform behind. The stone walls sometimes encased earthen banks and they were built from semi-dressed blocks in dry-stone construction. There are many hillforts encircling the Milfield basin, most of which can be visited. Of particular interest are the sites of Yeavering Bell, Humbleton Hill, West Hills and Dod Law.

British Revival
(AD410-AD550)

After the withdrawal of Roman armies in 410AD Britain soon reverted to a patchwork of petty kingdoms which were, to a large extent, based on the pre-Roman Iron Age boundaries. For half a century or so the 'tyrannies', as Gildas called them fought amongst each other as well as against Germanic mercenaries and invaders, Irish pirates and Pictish marauders. Despite the loss of its forces, the British were successful in driving out the invaders and raiding the lands of their hostile neighbours. The resurgence in native British culture during the 5th and early 6th centuries AD gave rise to a period of chivalrous values, success in war and the development of political systems based on kingship and patronage as well as a celebration of what we know now as Celtic arts. This included the production of exquisite works of craftsmanship, a vibrant oral and storytelling tradition, the writing of manuscripts in Latin and the popularity of bards who toured the courts of kings and Queens singing of their achievements and lamenting tales of woe and intrigue.

Coel the Old, the reputed British ruler of northern England after the Roman evacuation is the same 'Old king Cole' of nursery rhyme fame. The folk memory of his kingship is remembered in the rhyme:

> *"Old king Cole was a merry old soul*
> *and a merry old soul was he*
> *and he called for his pipe*
> *and he called for his bowl*
> *and he called for his fiddlers three"*

The Votadini lands centred on the Till valley became the British territory of Bryneich and was ruled by Coel's son Cunedda. After moving to Wales to take the kingship of Gwynedd Cunedda was replaced in Bryneich by Germanianus who made up for the loss of men by enlisting Anglian mercenaries.

Cunedda, the great grandfather of Maelgwyn, whose descendants ruled north Wales for eight centuries, sat in his royal hall at Ad Gefrin (Yeavering).

The roaring fire glowed bright in the hearth casting shadows over the dogs taking warmth from it. The bards strummed their music as the feast was served to the king and his counsel. The wild boar and piglet, goose, duck and beef were washed down with goblets of wine to the sound of laughter, boasts and toasts. The messenger sat next to Cunedda was intimidated by this great war leader.

He stood to take his leave from the table but in his nervousness jolted the table. Cunedda turned to the messenger and calmed him with "Sit down friend, we have much to discuss." The messenger had brought instructions from the overlord Vortigern for Cunedda to relocate to north Wales with part of his family and military force and drive out the Irish invaders and resettle the lands which would be his to keep. Cunedda knew this was a crucial decision that would decide the future of his Votadini kingdom and the security of western Britain.

The lure of wealth and land, pillage and war was too much a temptation for this warmonger who revelled in being honoured by his warriors, the subject of poems and above all the talk of Britain. He had already made up his mind but he was determined to make the messenger sweat before sending him back to Vortigern. He didn't want to appear too keen. Then he spoke, "I will take with me my wife and younger sons, together with 900 volunteer horsemen and their families, to Gwynedd. There we shall carve out a new kingdom and expel all invaders for now I have been given licence to do this unopposed by Lord Vortigern. We shall take the land and plunder of the invader for ourselves. And I promise you all, there will be wealth and power in this new kingdom for those who follow me. I entrust our homeland of the Votadini to my eldest son, Germanianus, who will inherit early what is already his by right. Messenger take this news with haste to Lord Vortigern for my lust for the invaders blood cannot wait."

A document from the collection of the monk Nennius tells us that in Wales Cunedda "expelled the Irish ...... with enormous slaughter, so that they never came back to live their again." A late Welsh poem formed from earlier poems tells of Cunedda as "Splendid in battle, with his nine hundred horse, Cunedda ...... the Lion." The early successes of the British which secured them from invaders was shortlived as the Germanic tribes stepped up their incursions in the east and south. It took until the end of

A bard sings tales of marriage between Christians and pagans and of feasting and merry-making.

These tales are set against the backdrop of warfare and pillage in these troubled times.

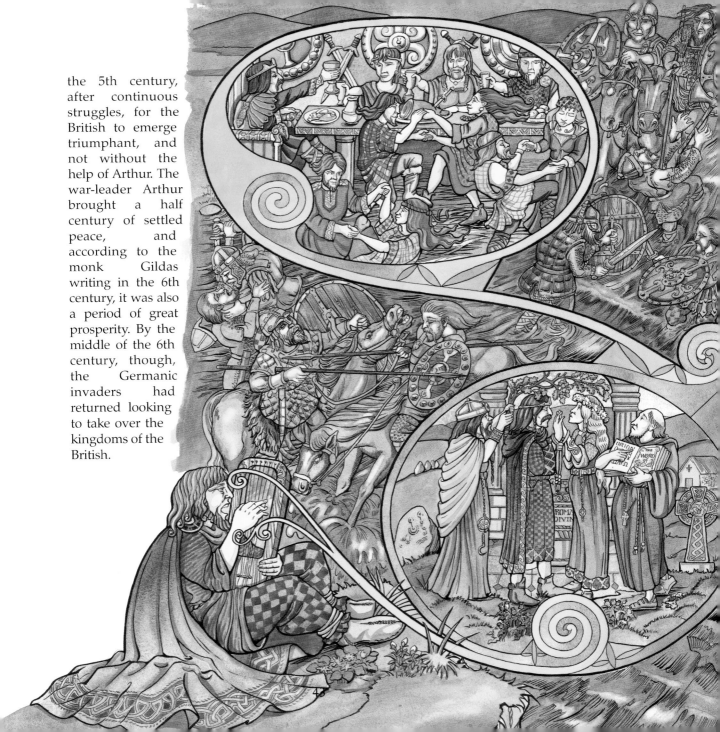

the 5th century, after continuous struggles, for the British to emerge triumphant, and not without the help of Arthur. The war-leader Arthur brought a half century of settled peace, and according to the monk Gildas writing in the 6th century, it was also a period of great prosperity. By the middle of the 6th century, though, the Germanic invaders had returned looking to take over the kingdoms of the British.

Anglo-Saxons
(AD550-AD1066)

When the Anglian kingdom of Bernicia was carved out in the mid 6th Century, nearly 150 years after the Romans left, they inherited a prosperous land stretching from the Lothians to the river Tees.

Probably the greatest of the early Anglo-Saxon kings was Edwin, a Deiran (modern East Yorkshire) by birth, who took the kingdom of Northumbria from Aethelfrith with the help of the great Raedwald of East Anglia. Bede tells us that under Edwin's reign he,

"brought under his sway all the territories inhabited either by English or Britons, an achievement unmatched by any previous English king. He also brought the Isles of Anglesey and Man under English rule."

After Edwin's death the royal centre of Ad Gefrin was moved to what is now modern Milfield. Bede tells us that, "This residence (Ad Gefrin) was abandoned by the later kings , who built another at a place called Maelmin." The site of Maelmin is situated to the east of the modern village of Milfield in the fields between the village and the river. It was surrounded by a massive double-palisade and contained great timber halls with perhaps a hundred or more houses and ancillary buildings. The reason for being located at Milfield was probably because this area forms the natural crossing point of the river Till at a pinch-point in the valley. The Maelmin Heritage Trail is built on the western edge of the town.

Edwin was a pagan but entered into a strategic alliance with the king of Kent by marriage to Ethelberga. Edwin struck a deal with Ethelberga's brother Eadbald that if he would betroth his sister in marriage to him then he would afford complete freedom to Ethelburga and her retinue to live and worship in accordance with Christian practice without hindrance and that he would be willing to take the religion of Christ, if on examination, his advisors thought it more holy than their own. Ethelberga was duly betrothed and sent to Edwin with the bishop Paulinus. After achieving a military victory and surrender from the West Saxons Edwin took instruction on the Christian faith from Paulinus.

A reconstruction of the royal town of Maelmin as viewed from the heritage trail site.

The position of the palisade and buildings are based on crop-marks visible on aerial photographs.

The pope, Boniface, also wrote to Edwin urging him to take up the faith and also wrote to queen Ethelberga asking her to exert her influence to bring her husband round to Christianity. Still Edwin would not be swayed by words alone. Edwin had had a vision when he was a hunted fugitive staying at Raedwald's court. Aethelfrith had offered Raedwald money to murder him and Raedwald was intending to do this. Edwin, saw a vision of a strange man who said he would change Raedwald's mind and make Edwin the greatest of all English kings but he must follow the path of salvation advised by the stranger when he saw this sign and then placed his hand on Edwin's head and blessed him.

After discussing this with Paulinus and his advisors Edwin professed acceptance of the Christian faith and was baptised in York. Then the king and queen travelled with Paulinus to their royal town of Ad Gefrin (Yeavering) where Paulinus spent 36 days baptising the Northumbrian people in the waters of the river Glen. It was during the time of the early Anglian kings of Northumbria that the Christian values, which have influenced the social, political and educational structures of the nation ever since, were established. By the later 7th century Northumbrian Christianity was well established and the clergymen Wilfrid, and later Willibrord, successfully took Christianity to northern Europe for the first time.

This is an account of real events handed down to us by Bede: *It was Easter Day in the year 626 and Edwin was seated in his timber hall with his advisors in attendance to receive a messenger from the king of the West Saxons. Edwin had been accepted as overlord of all England and Britain and as the Bretwalda he had an air of peace and calm about him after his years of surviving in exile when he was hunted relentlessly by Aethelfrith. Edwin greeted the messenger called Eumer who knelt in front of Edwin saying, "my king Cuichelm of the West Saxons brings you this" and with that drew a double-edged poisoned dagger from beneath his clothes and lunged for Edwin. In that instant Edwin recoiled from the assassin's assault and Edwin's friend Lilla threw himself in front of the assailant, for he had no shield, and took the full force of the thrust in his own body. The blow was delivered with such force that it still wounded the king through the body of the warrior. The assassin was attacked on all sides yet managed to kill another of the kings warriors named Fordhere. That same Easter night Edwin's wife gave birth to their daughter*

This scene depicts the arrival of the Angles when they land at Bamburgh.

The inset shows the pagan burial of one of the early Angle settlers with accompanying grave goods, rituals and chanting.

Eanfled. After recovering from his wound Edwin held his anger in check but quietly simmered with rage, for he was a contemplative man by nature. He told the Christian Paulinus, "if your God brings me victory over the West Saxons and delivers me the individuals who plotted this crime I will serve Christ." And as a pledge he gave his baby daughter to Paulinus for baptism as a token of his word. He set out with his force and took revenge. Bede tells us that he "marched against the West-Saxons, and in the ensuing campaign either slew or forced to surrender all those who had plotted his murder."

Ad Gefrin (Yeavering)

Archaeological excavations by Hope-Taylor (1977) have shown that the pagan temple at Ad Gefrin was a large rectangular wooden building 13m by 8m with ox-skulls set in a pit next to the east door. The remains of small huts found around the temple probably testify to its Christianisation as it was a stipulation of Pope Gregory that huts were to be constructed around pagan temples where ox sacrifices had taken place.

Adoration of the Magi

Another interesting clue to early Anglo-Saxon Christianity in the Milfield area can be found in the Church at Kirknewton. Here the Anglo-Saxon stone carving showing the adoration of the baby Jesus by the three wise men can be seen set into the Norman fabric of the church just before the apse. This carving is identical to the image on the Frank's casket – another early Anglo-Saxon Christian artefact. Perhaps this carving in Kirknewton church came from an earlier Anglo-Saxon church built at or near to the site where the present church stands?

During the 7th century a flowering of Northumbrian culture took place as a result of the fusion of British, Anglian and continental cultural traditions. Such great works as the Lindisfarne Gospels, the writings of Bede, teachings of St. Aidan, fine metalwork and architecture and the establishment of renowned centres of learning at Lindisfarne, Jarrow, and York are testament to this 'golden age'.